REFLECTIONS
Poems and Verse

Peter Questel

Copyright © 2024 by Peter Questel.

ISBN: 979-8-89465-096-8 (sc)
ISBN: 979-8-89465-097-5 (e)

All rights reserved. No part of this publication may be reproduced, distributed, or transmitted in any form or by any means, including photocopying, recording, or other electronic or mechanical methods, without the prior written permission of the author, except in the case of brief quotations embodied in critical reviews and certain other noncommercial uses permitted by copyright law.

Printed in the United States of America.

Integrity Publishing
39343 Harbor Hills Blvd Lady Lake, FL 32159

www.integrity-publishing.com

CONTENTS

Dedication vii
Acknowledgement. ix

PART 1

Love Is 3
The Power Of Love. 4
Love Them That Hurt You 5
Return Your Light. 6
A Universal Answer. 7
Looking Forward 8
Leave It Behind. 10
I Know Where I Am Going 11
To A Spiritual World. 12

PART 2

The Mystery Of Faith And Prayer. .15
Be Sure Of What You Want 16
Open The Gates Of Heaven 17
The Little Man 18
A Heavenly Thought. 20
Ozone. 21
News Of The World 22
News To The Lord (L.A). 24
Be Aware Of My Destructive Wrath 25
Spiritual Eyes 26

PART 3

Give Thanks And Praise 29
Appreciate, Honour And Cherish 30
All That's Good 31
The Wind 32
I Will Not Be Alone 33
The Glory Of Him 34
A Lovely Bank Holiday 35
A Day At Royal Ascot 36
Christmas 37
The Tree 38

PART 4

My Mother 41
Myra 42
Sister Angela 44
Sister Carol 45
Sister Susan 46
Abdul 47
Aunt Avis 48
Friends 49
Edme 50
Elsie 52
Father John 53
In Memory Of Our Beloved June 54
Jade 55
Heal 56

PART 5

Be Godly..61
Know Your God 62
No Man Is An Island 63
Delight And Grow Old..................................... 64
Time Is Just But A Day....................................66
Life Is No Big Deal..67
Women 69
Taken For Granted 70
What Goes Around Comes Around 71
The Reason You Are Here................................72
No God?...73
God Knows It 74
Open Your Eyes 75
Personality..76
Of Being 77

Dedication

This book is in memory of my grandparents, parents, brother John and sister Carol. Dedicated to my brothers and sisters: Angela, Philip, Sylvester, Susan and Michael.

Acknowledgement

My Heavenly Father who provided for me
the desires of my heart – without whom this book
would not be written.

Part 1

LOVE IS

Love is being in awe of the presence of hearing a bird sing
Love is the willingness to recognise that which is Divinely
　　real in each and every thing
Love is experiencing the bursting of the imaginary bubble
Love is finding the way to your fulfilment of purpose
Without the unnecessary trouble

Love is knowing who you Divinely are
Love is knowing what you are looking for is not too far
Love is knowing that which is spiritually, ultimately true
Love is knowing that it will be found in simple commonsense by you

Love is knowing that it's all there ever was, is and will be
Love is knowing that your Divinity is to be found in your humanity
Love is standing up for your own integrity
Love is knowing that your conscious experience yielded is Heavenly

Love is having and holding to the faith
Love is seeking ideas that illuminate
Love is presenting information to change someone's mind
Love is to be told off and still remain kind

Love is being non-judgemental and a witness for your brother
Love is being one with God and no other
Love is keeping resentment apart
Love is wet eyes and a soft heart

Love is underneath around and above
Love is all that we are made of
Love is a gift of God's free will
Love is the knowledge of silence and being still

Love is life, trust, mind, soul, principle and spirit
Love is the dynamic nature of God in it.

THE POWER OF LOVE

The power of love is the greatest of all
Through it many have risen and some will fall
Free to all with a good desire
Contagious, cold or as hot as fire

Such as it is I thought you must know
Taken to heart you will simply glow
Live to love, keep your heart in good health
Along the way past on the wealth

Look at the examples in every day
Meet someone and enjoy what they say
Like a fish it loves the water
So too a mother to her daughter

Like the waves that forever churn the sea
That's how much love is for you and me
Love and live and do good
Do it because you know you should

Love to show that you are just
Love to show it is a must
Generate love, see what you can do
Love is the word for me and you

Love the Creator and great Divine
Love for the sake of peace and mind
Lover of lovers and our friend
Spread love in His name, till the end.

LOVE THEM THAT HURT YOU

Love them that hurt you, turn a blind eye
It's not easy but still give it a try
There's more in your heart that you can give
Make it a habit in your life as you live

Think before you talk, envisage the cross
Keep calm and sturdy, never be at a loss
Dig deep for forgiveness for everyone
Bring out the true you and you have won

Take time and care as the day goes by
Radiant, joyful, don't even hurt a fly
Look out for who needs help in every day
Try and do good in your own little way

Remember disappointments are for the best
As odd as it seems it is a test
When a door closes in front of you
Move on quickly, the next, you will go through

Guide the young ones towards the light
Make them strong, merciful and bright
In these words, you hear me say
Do them religiously every day

So great is our maker of the world
He protects, warms and fulfils the soul
Strengthening us when we become weak
Inviting us to place our head at His feet

The goodness of God is abundantly seen
From Earth He created a human being
Reach and grasp for a place in His kingdom
We are truly His humble children.

RETURN YOUR LIGHT

Return your light that you showed me before
As darkness has returned and I see it no more
It's beautiful sparkle that shined every day
I'm lost without it; this I have to say

It's the first dull day for a very long while
Since within, that I did not smile
I know because you were not with me
I became distracted and I could not see

What a difference your lovely light does make
Holiness and joyfulness all for my sake
Return unto me your splendid light
My life is meaningless but with it so bright

Make me stronger for this lonely world
Strengthen and re-purify my Divine soul
Permit me not to close my eyes away from thee
Forgive, comfort and re-heal me

Send it down from way up above
As with it I'm forever in love
I deeply regret my wayward ways
Please return unto me my peaceful days.

A UNIVERSAL ANSWER

The answers of the universe remain firmly closed
An explosion of which all was disposed
We search for the reason of why we exist
No boundary undiscovered we forwardly persist

For what is the purpose that we are born for
Greatness, we have seen and anticipate more
As I marvel and ask myself why
The deepness of the ocean, the magnitude of the sky

With valleys of vegetation and forests of fruit trees
Mammals, birds, fishes and honey from the bees
A candle's flame in the dark of the night
A full moon radiantly shining bright

The sparkle of a diamond and its worth
The relief of a mother after giving birth
The movements of a petal as a flower slowly grows
The peacefulness of brilliant white snow

The innocence of a small sweet child
The sight of animals freely running wild
Reasoning is concealed with the one above
A new world He promises out of love

The answers are here and yet we cannot find
We need to be healed and to extend the mind
As we all play a part so precious indeed
But only through God will we ever succeed.

LOOKING FORWARD

It's the 2nd of May 1992
I look with anticipation for me and you
I'm interested in the co-existence of unity to flow
Not being too despondent as I see it slowly grow

The world still remains a troubled place
Answers I am sure stares us in the face
It is hard to believe there is still starvation
But wealth and prosperity in other nations

The lions have fallen in the Eastern Bloc
Bringing joy, celebration and with it shock
South Africa have just started their reform
It's a shame and a pity that it took so long

Saddam Hussein is still ruling with iron fist
George Bush defending saying it was no miss
Neo-Nazis are reforming in Berlin
The dollar is almost the equivalent of sterling

Conservatives have won in Britain again this year
Poor and less fortunate with ill feeling and fear
Race is still the main issue of the day
After all this time no one has found a way

A young man has killed both his parents in Italy
He becomes a hero, youth's shouting set him free
There's not even peace in the cricket we play
In the West Indies they have spoilt a historic day

Aids, a new disease, has appeared on the scene
I'm not sure everyone knows what it really means
Scientist are now saying that the world will end
But there's a Divine one and He's, our friend

They say that soon they will have life's secret
I'm not sure on this, but still, they can keep it
I continue to watch and ask myself why
But I can only be hopeful and try not to cry.

LEAVE IT BEHIND

Some experiences of going there are really no good
Sometimes you go there because you would
Of a recall for growth enthusiastically you should

You see reconnecting to this place there from
Polarises your development in moving on
Worst even it limits part of your definition

This place that I speak about just went away
The image is captured of the very day
What I speak of is in your head and also in your way

One might remember someone growing up being small
People with their perceptions saying you are not very tall
Retained convictions would have served no good purpose at all

An ignorant teacher says boy you can't do the math
And further more here's for you a dunce's cap
A possible career in number, well that's the end of that

You knew a guy in school and he was a known twit
Every time you saw him you avoided and had a fit
Thirty years has gone by would you now with him sit

This place gives a bad assessment of what you think you are
Don't let it inhibit you to reach in your quest quite far
The moments that have gone are now ajar

By all means improve it and make it sharp and nice
If you want to remember facts and details in life
Then take daily a quarter tea spoon of Allspice

Now that thing of the mind which imprisons you and me
And holds back the progress to our Real destiny
Is in what we are drawing from our memory.

I KNOW WHERE I AM GOING

I was lost
But now I'm found
I searched for the truth
And was enlightened
My heart was empty
But now I know love
My house was without light
But now brightness shines forever
I was afraid
And now I know no fear
I was unsure of my path
But now I know where I am going.

TO A SPIRITUAL WORLD

I am dead to this world
Yet I'm alive to the next
My body still lives
But my mind is foreign to it
And it waits for my body
For then I will be able to rest
My body cannot enter
For where I am going
It's to a spiritual world.

Part 2

THE MYSTERY OF FAITH AND PRAYER

Know the mystery of faith and prayer
Be still, listen, open eye and ear
Speak to Him, ask for his pardon
It is the route to His Heavenly Garden

Give our Lord some time of day
For He will clear your path and way
Release unto Him what is due
He will surely make you anew

Where all is still and no darkness is
A place beyond belief and it's all His
To one and all He opens His arms
Protecting and keeping us fully charmed.

With wings He will give us so we can fly
And the beauty of all we will never die
Imagine how nice that it could be
Singing His praises, being totally free

Jesus, Lord, Saviour, Superstar
Let us all be wherever you are
Your death for us eternal life
To believe truly in Jesus Christ

How faithful you are our never-ending love
So far, far away, up above
We hail your name rightfully deserve
Please have all our places kindly reserved.

BE SURE OF WHAT YOU WANT

Be sure of what you want from our maker
Be it good, He will give, for He is the creator
Pray sincerely and be careful what you say
You do not want to live to regret every day

Ask for something that you can live to
Be sure you want it and be very true
Ask Him to show you the just way
Remember with sacrifices you must pay

Do not be afraid, ask to walk in His path
Not much is needed and no special art
It's a simple life He wants us to live
All that's needed is to be good and give

Although it's difficult forsaking your pleasures
And so unbelievable are the unforeseen treasures
The way of the Father is simple indeed
Go to Him and tell Him your needs.

OPEN THE GATES OF HEAVEN

Lord open the gates of Heaven for me
So, I can open my eyes and see
The pleasures that you have for me in store
It's beyond imagination of this, I am sure

Make my path as smooth as can be
As I know I have confidence in thee
My existence on Earth is trying indeed
But I know in time I will succeed

I have troubles in my heart but I know you are there
I stay calm and content and I have no fear
I know that I'm here to spread your word
And in truth's search it's the best I've heard

I know that through you I will do my best
And I know you will give me plenty rest
I have faith with hope and I earnestly pray
That I will surely meet you one day

For when you come with your great hand
To collect all the pieces of your religious band
For I know all who have answered to your call
Will enjoy the greatest journey of all.

THE LITTLE MAN

There's a little man inside of you
Who knows what you ought to do
He is eager to show you the way
If only you'll let him have a say

He won't speak to you
If you don't want him to
Patiently he awaits your call
Independently available to all

He's been with you all the time
On the other side of your mind
It could be a she, to think of it
And all for your total benefit

There's transformation to be had
They do want you to be glad
If you invite, they will receive
You will make them infinitely pleased

The challenge is a great one
To you, daughter or son
There's an obstacle you should know
It's called the ego

He's a wretch and a no good
But control, yes, he certainly could
Have no fear of this empty space
Your originality is from a much higher place

If you get rid of this useless idea
You could not foresee what would appear
There would be only recognition of the past
As you isolate and create a cask

Then, you will instantly glow
Presently be and know
Gloriously you'll become one
With the movement of Creation.

A HEAVENLY THOUGHT

Have you ever wondered
How wonderful a thought could be
Like floating effortlessly, in space and in the sea.
A hero, star, saint, a dolphin, a bee?
What would you want to see?
Who would you be?

Perhaps, you may want to fly,
Deep from within the vast blue sky.
Would you want to be confident, strong and tall.
Or maybe, know the understanding of the bird's call
You could for a day be a king
A song you could write, perform and sing

Who would you visit?
Where would you go?
What do you think you'll need to know?
If you thought, your thought could be true
Would this differ in what you do?

Would you not want to think without much
As even a blink, just for one day
You hear the Angels say,
'Come with us
For we will show you the way.'

OZONE

New predictions of scientists are expressed today
In short here is some of what they have to say
Fiery rings from above have sparked another ozone alert
A huge increase in heat may eventually choke the earth

A deep hole has been carved in the ozone shield they say
Which protects the Earth's surface from the sun's deadly ray
Chemicals is the cause used in aerosols, fridges and foams
So, imagine destroying the world in your own home

Man made gasses chlorine and bromine does most damage
It's bleak for the 21st century, only God knows how we will manage
Even an animal is under scrutiny now
Smelly methane gas produced by a grazing cow

They say it's intensifying with every year
And some have said all this is hot air
Scientist have established and have the answer
But did predict a 26% increase in skin cancer

So, we are warming the planet with our pollution
And yet at hand there is a solution
They advise to handle the world with extreme care
To lift this disturbing living fear

Mankind tested and proven with the human race
The threat of the planet being attacked from outer space
Environmental disasters and the horrifying heat
Optimism yes, but in the new, I have booked a seat.

NEWS OF THE WORLD

Lord, once again I'm here to say
All that's new and happened today
There is still no peace in Jerusalem
Among Jews, Christians and Muslims only confusion

In Britain a bishop has confessed to having a love child
Utilizing church funds effortlessly with a smile
We have here a prophet called the son of God
He's got one of his disciples pregnant, Lord

'Basic Instinct', a new movie on the scene
Glorifying lust but they say it's meant to be clean
Canonization is now being speeded up
But some good men still getting the chop

The war of the Gulf with the friendly fire
Pentagon or the pilots, they say someone is a liar
The Catholic Church is rethinking about contraceptives
They say people lives in the Third World are not in prospective

Trouble has arisen in the East in Bangkok
Prodemocracy riots, I believe it's quite hot
We can now produce chickens in half the time
Pigs we can also do in a new design

In space we can man handle a satellite
Preset it and further send it to a new height
Summer has come extremely early this year
One hundred degrees or more is feared

I met a fellow who does not believe in the cross
He said he reads the Bible, but I told him to get lost
Finally, there is a new optimism in the air
More and more people are turning to prayer

Goodbye for now my dearest friend
Soon I hope to speak to you again
Hopefully it will contain something good
I have lots of faith and I know you would.

NEWS TO THE LORD (L.A.)

Lord as I sat and watch the news
I am sad, shocked and so confuse
I could not believe that in this day and age
People seeking justice and so filled with rage

They were crowds angry at the elite
Men beating each other as they meet
Everything being destroyed and left to burn
Poor and oppressed screaming it's our turn

Can we ever look forward on Earth for peace
Or is this madness never to cease
I speak of the City of Angels in the USA
God only knows what's to happen today

A land promised of so much opportunity
With only a fraction of community
A place so blessed with riches and good soil
Wheat, ballistic missiles, rockets and oil

Divided between the rich and poor
Peace, togetherness, mercy no more
They spend billions seeking a new world
Leaving millions destitute, unloved and cold

Man here on Earth can he rectify his problem
Or is he looking for extra-terrestrial life to solve them
It's the same everywhere you go and seek
Multitudes unhappy, lost and terribly weak

Is it a sign that you may soon come
Or is it us, the answers must come from
The answer is here for all to see
We can only be happy with unity.

BE AWARE OF MY DESTRUCTIVE WRATH

I will forever be your friend
To serve and love you till the end
With kindness I will keep for you
Forgiveness always, I will be true

Simplicity and patience are bestowed in me
Modesty and understanding are desired of thee
Humility and innocence are what I am
Hurt me, and I will sing to you a psalm

My soul is filled with sanctifying grace
Evil I will not permit in any place
Mildness is imbedded in my mind
I will protect you time and time

I live with faith and for charity
Abstinence and discipline are my priority
Love I live for now, as before
I expect no less, of this, be sure

For all of these I relentlessly keep
Annoy me not, for I'll make you weep
Place yourself within my path
And be aware of my destructive wrath.

SPIRITUAL EYES

Let not your eyes be closed
But open them anew
And be drawn into the spiritual energy
Of the powerful unifying influence
So that you can see unveiled
Gaining abundantly
In Divine love and Divine law
Manifesting soul satisfying experiences
Equipped to overcome evil with good
Fear, anger, jealousy and suspicion
Replaced by matchless love and mutual trust
Ennobling the life of which you live
In this short span of mortal moments
Seeking individual souls with unswerving determination
For the brothers and sisters fellowship of living worship
Reaping spiritual credits for the reward of the ages
To witness truth, beauty and sublime goodness.

Part 3

GIVE THANKS AND PRAISE

Give thanks and praise to God
Father, king and our Lord
Freely He gives us this day
Simply to follow in his way

He lights the darkness of the sky
Holy priest of the most high
Patiently He remains in every heart
Helping to ignite that little spark

Ever forgiving our daily sins
With its comfort to us it brings
To enter into His holy universe
Unrighteousness must be reverse

Prepare sincerely for His new world
Cleanse and purify your soul
The reward of our Father is immensely great
For this the reason He did create

Material things here on this earth
In our Father's kingdom has no worth
Show mercy and kindness to one and all
Have faith, for you too, will be called.

APPRECIATE, HONOUR AND CHERISH

Miraculous Infant Jesus
As always, you're sweet to me
How I've turned my back
Away from loving thee

I know you guide me always
Yet I neglect you ever so much
Although I know all that's needed
Is a simple little touch

You are my reason for living
And I treat you second best
I live my life so freely
And often failing in my tests

I am but only human
And you are so Divine
I am praying daily
For your world to be mine

So gentle, peaceful and graceful
Forever forgiving one and all
I am here for you Infant Jesus
For whenever you choose to call.

ALL THAT'S GOOD

Blessed be your name Jesus
For in you I'm patient
I am warm in your love
Comforted in your household
Filled in your holiness
I'm never alone or without
For you are always with me
I fear nothing
For you are strength itself
As I am born to serve you
Loving all in my ways
Disregarding sin
With inspired reason
My time here is only but short
But through you
My life will be forever
What task awaits me
Of your glorious master plan
Eagerly I stay contented
For soon I will see all that's good.

THE WIND

The Wind Whips through the Window
Gushing Sweet Feelings
Equilibration of Mind and Body
A New Phase of Day New Birth
Sweeper of Old
Majestically Orchestrated
Precise as if Ordained
Tenderly Hums its Lullaby
Humility to Put Sleep to Child
Humour to Impede
Carrier of Flights
Symbol of Mystique
Canny Benevolence
Fatherly Orderer of Oceans
Swiftly Engulfing Prey
With Strength of Universal Might
Keeper of the Spheres
Searching Belligerently
Driver and Destroyer of Life
Invisibility of Destiny
Wind of Joy Wind of Pain
Wind of Content Wind of Spirit
Wind of Soul Wind of Firmament
Wind of Heaven's breath.

I WILL NOT BE ALONE

When I die
Please do not cry
For you will make me sad
But rest assured I will be glad
Because I will be gone to His new world
Taking with me my humble soul
So, when you think of me
Look to the sky and see
The boarders of my Father's home
And be happy to know
That I will not be alone.

THE GLORY OF HIM

They want you to be happy today
As they are delighting in your love
Mum and Dad are within your stillness
All because of the One above
In your quietness you will feel their pressure
The ego is to be ignored today
And the blessings, solitude and joy
Will never go away
They miss you as much as you miss them
But they have no regrets or fear
Because at a moment's notice
With open eyes they see you here
They are now, all knowing
And they are content with their child
Especially as they are experiencing Real love
Through the clouds they peep with a cheeky smile
So, cheer up Mrs Mc Sperrin
Say a prayer and sing a hymn
Your parents are in spirit
Tenderly attended by Angels
And the Glory of Him.

A LOVELY BANK HOLIDAY

The sun is out in its glory
Beaming its beautiful ray
Birds are busily singing
Most, I am sure, at play

Clouds are moving slowly
But yet, they seem so still
Breeze swaying the trees
All in nature's will

The greenery seems much greener
As it never did before
Seagulls in their splendour
On the beach, sea and shore

Excitement fills the atmosphere
In the streets, shops and parks
Music playing loudly
Night parties are soon to start

The heat is less intensified
As the sun slowly fades away
Then comes the moon and stars
To enter and have their say

The sky is now fully alit
Beautiful in every way
Everyone so grateful
For a lovely Bank Holiday.

A DAY AT ROYAL ASCOT

A day at Royal Ascot aristocracy is on the scene
Rich and with Royalty all in their gleam
The sun's light sparkles and breeze quite sweet
People in their glory looking all so neat

Sir of this and Lord of that
Elegant ladies jolly with chat
Some in white, yellow and in pink
Gentlemen with top hats and tails and with drink

Flowers in their radiance almost everywhere
Some sitting nicely on the ladies' hair
Horses parading with such majestic grace
Anxiety fills the air as they prepare to race

The crowds are most sociable they say it's the place to be
With caviar and champagne after a cup of tea
Strawberries and ice cream, sliced cucumber with salmon
You can win, lose or be merry before the day is done

Money spending so lavishly and without much care
Everyone in paradise with good cheer everywhere
A glorious yearly spectacle you will be amazed to see
Although all are welcome it may not suit you or me

The day unfolds lazily most enjoyed their pleasure
Others may have had much more than their measure
All in all, what splendour and seemingly good fun
Here in this land of England can you so delight in the sun.

CHRISTMAS

Prepare ye well for the coming of the season
There's joy to be had and with it good reason
So, make way wholeheartedly for this great feast
It's time of goodwill and a gentle peace

You're got the cards, presents and the meat
Cake and cream added for the splendid treat
The house is kept clean, you sweep, mop and shine it well
A visit you may have and good of you they should tell

The candles are lit
And you switch on the decorative lights
Within is the gift of the Holy Spirit
Who blesses the room and makes it bright

Over indulged and now ready for a TV repeat
Drink in hand, lazily you slide into your seat
The shepherds knew and the wise men followed the star
It's because of them Divinely so, you are

Enjoy the festive time
Here on Earth
But remember and reflect on
The importance of our Saviour's birth.

THE TREE

The tree stands there
Unconcerned upright rigid
Solid as a rock
Testament of time
Observing and displaying
Different attires
Undressed in winter
Naked for all to see
Unashamed being of pure nature
Dry cold frozen frame
Rooted to the Earth
Like a sturdy palm timber
Silent she stands
Stems and branches
Like a giant with one thousand hands
Loving speechless organism
With mechanism defying reason
Lightly dressed with
Leaves in abundance
Dancing in the passing winds
Shimmering dense symmetrical beauty
Flowers like mini planets
Dawns her Ceremonial gown in summer
Elegantly sways and swirls
Like a carnival queen of a band
Autumn's colour completes its circle
Portraying characteristics of the Supreme.

Part 4

MY MOTHER

Thanks to you mother which I give this day
It's within my heart I feel I must say
The seeds that you sow, are now to reap
Thanks for the lessons and our keep

Blessed are you and so divine
Look at your children all lovely and kind
We never had much but were always fill
It's because of you and your very strong will

So good was your faith that you gave to us
All so simple and without much fuss
You taught us a lot and to stand alone
And yet your door remained open at home

Thanks for the kindness, it's out of this world
My wish for you to live until I grew old
May God grant you what you may desire
Good health, long life and a place in His empire.

MYRA

You left with such an incredible speed
Not knowing how much you were still in need
Like a flash straight out of the sky
Without warning or farewell you just died

Our Earthly Angel so long our friend
Will we not see you?
I hope, we will again.
The memories you left us to recall and endure
We would have wanted many, many, many more

You remember the carnival time the man bust through the door
We thought we were in for trouble and even more
Papa was having his early morning tea
When all of a sudden, a man flew in faster than a bee

He was painted black with a tail and a fork in his hand
But instead turned around and headed back in the band
This time you hid us well out of the way
Right under the Chapel where you would pray

You remember the night you were sewing late near the door
A man peeped through the jalousie and your eyes made four
You yelled out with such an electrifying scream
The man disappeared and was never again seen

You remember the time Boysie came with the dog bite
He was calm and cool but what a sore sight
Boysie was bitten from head to toe
He said he went by some people he didn't know

My heart bleeds for your loving voice
I feel empty and it's not my choice
But I know that from within your death
There is life and I will draw a new breath

Thank you for the lessons of wisdom of the day
Thank you for the kindness and showing the way
I give thanks and praise to the Lord above
For the presence and longevity of your love

Today, I dedicate to you
I speak from the heart
Amusingly, frank, but true.

In loving memory of my mother Myra Questel 24/01/2003

SISTER ANGELA

I cannot think of many things
That would give me so much pleasure
Than my wonderful years
The memories of you, I do treasure

Angela, so romantic
A woman heavenly blessed
Graceful and charming
With a will to do her best

I look back so clearly
Of you being so true
I remember you this day
And devote it all to you

Brown eyes so beautiful
Bringing good cheer to every room
As I remember
How, my days were gone too soon

With your sweet smiling appearance
So majestic and divine
Whenever I think of thee
Only gladness comes to mind.

SISTER CAROL

Oh, sister of mercy and humility
If ever there was one
What greatness we shared
And with it lots of fun

Carol, what sweet joy
It is of the name
As you have lived
With so much toil and pain

The light that now shines upon you
May it be the quest that you seek
Be true, and yours to keep

For one with such gentle heart
Gracefully shall you some day
Ascend to your Father
And there have rest and stay.

SISTER SUSAN

Susan of good virtue
This I say of you
I speak for all
My brothers and sisters too.

Oh, what Heavenly bliss
The thought of thee
I give thanks
Simple with a kiss.

Always up bright and firm
Secure indeed
Beautiful sweet child
Godly seed.

We had joy in our fights
And in our play
I cherish our youth
I give thanks today.

What wonderful comfort
You did give
Forever in my heart
Your name shall live.

ABDUL

A sense of emptiness looms within
A sense of loss has come
A gentle giant has gone away
His journey here a remarkable one

Converted to a new faith
He's now returned to his home
Leaving many feeling
Helpless, astonished and alone

Thank you for the gift that you
Left us behind
The simplicity of life
Of which you defined

The double-edged sword of life
Is evident to see
Joy and sorrow experienced
In the minds of you and me

The service that you have given
To so many in your time
Is imprinted throughout the universe
And within their minds

You believed in the Prophet
So, your rewards are due
Where ever you are Abdul
Surely, clothed in glory, anew.

Dedicated to my loving brother John Questel: aka Abdul Barr 02/01/09

AUNT AVIS

Sweet Aunt Avis, how I love thee so
Far, far away from the land I let go
Divine and happy the remembrance of thee
How I long for a spirit, like yours within me

At Christmas you came bringing lots of gifts
Leaving us all joyfully and with a kiss
So great your kindness that you let flow
Whenever we saw you what a beautiful glow

The goodness of your heart you gave to the poor
And still you gave freely if they wanted more
Sick, elderly, destitute and the blind
Lord knows you gave all peace of mind

With your Holy excursions that we all went
Surely you were Heavenly sent
Your power of faith and of prayer
May God bless you forever and keep you near.

FRIENDS

What is a friend?
A friend is one of God's gifts to mankind
They are the pilots of the journey of life
They are:
Divine
Lights in the dark
The main ingredient of love
Blessings of the Earth
Human flowers
Earthly Angels, without wings
More valuable than diamonds or pearls
The practicality of love
A source of life's external
Two hearts entwined
Real Love
There, in every moment of time
And our fallen friends, they live in the natural way.

EDME

It was on the 46th Independence Day
That your life here on Earth came to an end
And also 40 years of the experiences
Of you being a friend

You're missed my fellow brethren
Sadness fills the atmosphere
But I know in the consciousness
I can still feel you near

A man of such trusted position
With insight that was out of this world
Your kindness to your fellow man
The stories will forever be told

Elegance was your forte
Compassion you were true
Humility your fortune
Wisdom was God's gift here for you

Blessed with a limitless talent
Drummer and bugler as a cadet in your land
Added to your many sweet notes
Played in your favourite steel band

No day will pass not thought of
No weather will prevail
No man on your Trinidad Island
Can add injury to your name

I envisage and comprehend
As you gracefully lived here on Earth
What the Father has given you
And what you are now worth

I admit this is written
With a tear at the eye
But there's joy in the solitude
As I view a star in the dark sky.

Dedicated to my dear friend, Edme Gibbons 31/08/08

ELSIE

In such a short time
That I have known you
The many moments
All being so true

The memories so much to
Cherish and to recall
You were friend and companion
To many and all

The Angels are delighted
To have you back
But for us your presence
Is what we need but would lack

You have your Divined, deserved rest
And we will strive to follow your path
Of the fulfilments
You brought to each and every heart

You are now far away
Yet we still feel you are here
Elsie my dear daily
For you, we shall dedicate a prayer.

Dedicated to Elsie

FATHER JOHN

It's with joy and sadness
That today we celebrate with
You Father John
Chosen to serve as God's own son

We thank you Father
For the many Holy moments
Instilled in our hearts we share
Forever, we hold them there

Your guidance of school and community
From baby to the aged
Together experiencing, the glory of love
With showers of blessings from God above

We know that in our Father's house
There are multitudes of rooms
One rightfully reserved for you
With an eternal celestial view.

Dedicated to Father John

IN MEMORY OF OUR BELOVED JUNE

When I think of thee only gladness comes to my mind
Beautiful in appearance with an engaging smile
A personality that was out of this world
Truly you were here on Earth as a representative of the Divine

Aunt Avis knew that you were to be called June
The same month that Gabriel appeared to Elizabeth
To give the news of her oncoming son
In the year 8 B.C. just about noon

I remember so vividly the many memories of you
I thank the Father from above
For the love of which you displayed
As you have answered my many requests and being all so true

As you ascend the Heavenly circles towards Paradise
The Angels and the Celestial host are celebrating
Your task here is now done
For soon you shall be embraced by Jesus Christ

We are now left without your unrelenting grace
The pain and sorrow are all too much to bear
But we know that as you enter the spiritual world
There you shall have your rest in the Holiest Place.

JADE

Dear Jesus,
In the season of goodwill, in the near hour of your rebirth
We ask you to intercede on behalf of our class Angel Jade
We offer our prayer to the God of the highest Heaven
Let us experience Jade's gift blossomed
Make her as new as when you first made her
In perfection

Let her continue to grace our corridors, the playground
And in the classroom as there is an absence of love
Heal her quickly for she brings with her a peace within
Wherever placed

Our hearts are sorrowed and eyes are softened
Anxiety remains while our tears run freely
Let Jade's parents and all at school
Continue to enjoy the joy of her love
Let her light shine brightly, renew her strength
Eliminate her anguish, make her healed
This we ask of you, Jesus

Our love, faith and our passion in you
Will never cease
Because we believe
Thank you, Jesus,
As we await eagerly
Like humble children
The celebration of God's gift to the World.

HEAL

Love your body with an enduring passion
Deprive not the world of the whole gift of you
It is the visibility and tangibility of your presence
Identifying your individuality perfectly, as a Divine essence

Love will see your body manifesting greater and greater harmony
Let not your body behave improperly due to tension
Modify and harmonise your attitude to the fact
Immediately abandon the stance of attack

Spiritually your thoughts you must rearrange
Let not the function appear to be distorted
Honouring your attitude would make it gel
Love will seal it and make it well

The fear that's at hand is at odds with you
Know that the healing takes place in the awareness
A spontaneous connection with your heart will surely do
Take this affirmation to be true

Shift from fear to the attitude of love
Know that the healing will occur
With your heart experiencing
The inner threshold where Angels tenderly sing

Be the genuine expression of God which is what you are
Enter the place where help awaits
Ask to be healed and anticipate it gained
The eradication and destruction of what seemingly was pain

Visit this void as you are lovingly invited
With guidance you will reach this place of excellence
Just ask for the direction of the map
And you will find what's known as the Gap

No thoughts are needed here
To make conscious contact with God
To seek in the stillness of the invisible force
Within the inner blank screen of your mind
In the space between your thoughts
Healing shall you there find.

Dedicated to my loving brother Michael

Part 5

BE GODLY

Be good to your parents, brothers and sisters too
For it will be returned unto you
Give unto all freely if they need
Imbedded in you is a Godly seed

Share all your blessings from above
He has made us out of pure love
Give all you can, more, if you have to do
It's in God's name and He won't neglect you

Shine bright, and be happy wherever you are
Stand up and be counted, reach for a star
Touch and heal someone if you can
It will bring you nearer to the promised land

God is our Father and master of all
Do good and wait for his Heavenly call
Be gentle and as sweet as a lamb
Strong and confident with a bible in hand

Enjoy the simple pleasures in your life
Strive to be like Jesus Christ
Be thankful and sing aloud His name
Never ever should you be ashamed

Be good to yourself, daily say a prayer
In God, do trust and you will have no fear
The power of God is almighty indeed
Believe in Him, there is nothing else you need.

KNOW YOUR GOD

Know your God and be sure it is Him
No need to go far for He sleeps within
Ruler of the sea, sun, moon and sky
Creator of all things, even you and I

Light of lightness with a heart of gold
For centuries the story is still being told
Guard of truth all time and space
Lord and super human of our race

Almighty of almighty, judge of all
On his word only, shall all creation fall
Father of goodness with a psalm in hand
Be all worthy, He is king of the lamb

In blinding armoury as He will come
And to his word all will be done
Make no mistake of what you will see
Only the evil shall have fear of thee

For when He comes with the sharpest blade
All good men will not be afraid
For of the God of material things
It is he, with sinfulness he brings

The lover of wrong doings, with a heart of stone
He would want you for one of his own
False promises he offers you so bold
In the interest of your very own soul.

NO MAN IS AN ISLAND

No man is an island in history and present time
The good, the bad and the ugly none to find
Adam our first fore father lived for over nine hundred years
Eve and all his grandchildren still wept many tears

As the world is here today but maybe gone tomorrow
So too will all elements and creatures will follow
Even Samson so strong with so much will
But as the scripture says his time was soon fulfilled

As the universe was designed from the start
The moon, sun, stars and water being the first part
Everyone has his hour and an avenue
So, participation is anticipated from even me or you

Whether a king, scholar or a brute
From your endeavours so shall you bear your fruit
Rich, the professional or a priest who didn't give
Judgement is scaled to the life you live

So, if nothing became something
Then could not something become nothing
Respect then unto everyone as all will have a part to play
And remember that every dog will have its day.

DELIGHT AND GROW OLD

Delight in yourself as you age and grow old
The truth of life is within one's own soul
Take hold of your stock and show them the way
Teach them the secret that's in every day

Don't dwell of wrongs done before
Think of God, do good and more
Whenever you are low and you need a high
Look straight up beyond towards the sky

Keep your heart filled with love
This you will share with the one above
Be thankful for the life you lived
It's out of love He did give

Resist the temptation to preserve your life
There is nothing better than to meet Christ
Imagine what a world this would be
If everyone lived to five hundred and three

No room to manoeuvre, no place to play
Nothing new to look forward to in a new day
No new blood or faces in our world
Just health and wealth so I've been told.

As man progresses from A to B
He forgets quickly life's a learning tree
If the Lord wanted us to live on Earth forever
Surely, He would have made us much more clever

Still living with horror and fear
Some people do it year after year
We are only eight away from two thousand years
Haven't we seen enough trouble and tears

You may be one of the chosen few
Man here on earth promise life anew
Every man to his own then unto his son
I'll wait for Heaven, there, I will be redone.

TIME IS JUST BUT A DAY

Time is just but a day
Madness, I hear someone say
Yet, they can't remember much of their earlier age
All that was is now just a page

Time is just but a day
Crazy, she says it is in no way
Nine months it took to give birth
And how much is that now worth

Time is just but a day
Insane, some may say
You go on a two-week vacation
And in an instant, it's gone

Time, the present moment or now
Could it ever just simply go?
And where did it come from
Do you know?

LIFE IS NO BIG DEAL

I met a man the other day and this is what he had to say
He said that life is not what it really is: it's no big deal
And furthermore, he said to me, that it is not even real
I was baffled by this man's words: but who am I to preach
This man had a lot to say so I remained silent in my speech

Multitudes of people are actively sleeping now, here on Earth
Some have reduced themselves of any self-worth
They carry on in their day as if they were blind
They are so busy that they rarely use purposefully their mind
Often, opportunities are wasted due to the unkindness of man
When all that's needed is a helping or willing hand
They have forgotten that they are from the Divine
And by their nature they are all kind

I remained in my quiet state and listened intensively
He was silent for a while and then said this to me:
There is a way you know, how to get out of this dream
With simplicity you can again, become clean
This is something you do every single day
Yet many are still not finding the way
They struggle by themselves to see what they could gain
But often in their lives endure recurring pain
There are of course the many happy times
Measured to the sound of chimes

He then said that they have got it all wrong
Something new is being created and has to be sung
One without the 'me' and 'me'
All things then, they will abundantly see
The message is pure, simple and clear
From beyond and within our sphere
But no distance far away
It's from within you to have a say

He then mentioned the Source of which we all have a guide
With this he says, eyes may see what's really inside
He then spoke of Heaven, not of when you die
And not even the one that is referred to in the sky
He said to enter this blissful place is childish indeed
All you need to do is return to your Godly seed
Uncover the veil that covers your face
Instantaneously, you will return to your eternal grace

I was confused about this daily chore
And I asked him to explain some more
He said my friend the negativity must stop
All we have to do is………..Wake Up!

WOMEN

A beautiful companion which God made of man
Created to be together by His great hand
So sensual and fruitful as they can be
Some are not worthy of you or me

Remember that beauty lies in the heart
So do give all an equal start
Always treat them with kindness and due respect
It's the recipe for no regret

Beware of the sparkle in their eye
It can cause weakness and make you lie
Gentle are the ones who are always quiet
It's no guarantee there won't be a riot

See them walking in the street
Looking lovely and really sweet
Tall, short, black or white
They are all a pleasant sight

Keep away from the ones who are loud
They are the first you will see in a crowd
Also, the ones who like to roam
It's not nice having one at home

Blessed are they who have a good one
Prosperity awaits and lots of fun
Honour and cherish your own too
With modesty be gentle and be true

If you're without and you eventually meet
Give thanks for the kindness of this lovely treat
But if you're unlucky and haven't found love
Chastity is of Divinity up above.

TAKEN FOR GRANTED

Take your life not for granted
Our Creator would not have wanted
Do not think evil, not even mention
Instead seek and receive full redemption

Turn away from society's sinfulness
Only in this way can you gain fullness
Respect the prophet's ideology
Be sure they owe you no apology

Disregard others if they think you are extreme
Remember to hold your self esteem
For some day all would be equal
It seems to me, perfectly logical

Do not always think the same
It's a question of change or blame
For one day you will prepare for rain
Only to find you are deceived again

Unanswered questions you will find in your quest
But keep your beliefs and try your best
Life can be cruel and sometimes mean
But life is much larger than what it seems.

WHAT GOES AROUND COMES AROUND

As the world circles in its path
So, the seasons follow with majestic art
Everything fixed onto its course
People living daily feeling the force

But it looks like that whatever you do
It somehow returns unto you
So do take heed to what I say
Live life not to regret it later someday

Treat others as you would like to be treated
Never have anyone say that you have cheated
Don't speak peace with your tongue
While in your heart there is only wrong

Respect yourself and your parents too
It's the foundation of which you came through
Help the unfortunate as you continue on your road
Later in life yours might be a heavier load

Don't do evil keep away from it please
In the place of limitless darkness there is no ease
Think of the children perverseness do them not
Woe unto you if you find it terribly hot.

THE REASON YOU ARE HERE

The master showed clearly
From his point of view
To behold the truth
And accept the new

Live and love boldly
Be conscious of the fact
Your brothers and sisters
Create there to be no lack

Eyes wide open
In the light of the day
No coincidence to unfold
That may sway your way

If a man asks for a dollar
Give him two
The mystery of this
Cannot be solved by you

Share your gifts
And share them well
Enhancing in personality
Within the Cosmos you will swell

Avoid the action
Of doing a fancy curve
The reason you are here
Is simply, to serve.

NO GOD?

What! He says: There is no God!
And when he dies there will be
Nothing left, Lord

You mean we are here by chance?
How did this happen?
Were our forefathers apes?

You mean we have no soul
No spirit, no belonging?
So how did we get here?

If there is no God
Who upholds the sun, moon and the stars?
There is no controller, you say

And why is the universe expanding?
Where did it come from?
And where is it going?

Who has these answers?
Is there an answer?
Yes, yes. I say

God is alive and lives in everyday
You can't see him, but in the silence
You may feel his presence

And as the sun will rise tomorrow
He will be there within with Angels,
Who records everything.

GOD KNOWS IT

The Lord knows our outcomes
He knows the fruits that we will bear
We do not know it
Yet, we are the pilots of our own individual destinies
God invites us to experience the Paradise Embrace
He grants us free will
Because the Lord is boundless in mercy
Are you going to respond to His Supreme Mandate?
'Be you perfect, even as I am perfect'
To strive onward to the attainment of higher levels of spiritual values
Or are you to be judged spiritually spent and be as you never were?
Only through the Heavenly Father
Can our souls be enlightened and nourished
And with the use of clear thinking in our minds
We will know the truth, the True reality,
And the Love.

OPEN YOUR EYES

Tomorrow is yet to come
And yesterday has gone
So, for today
For God's sake: Have some fun

If you feel bad at present
Life is seriously kind
And know that happiness
Is a state of mind

Look at nature
See the smiling trees
Insects and birds are busy
At work too are the bees

There's no time for sadness
Fill your heart with joy
And treat each second
Like you would with a treasured toy

Share your smile with others
Say something nice to someone
And if you are still feeling low
Then eat a large raw onion.

PERSONALITY

Not self-centred nor isolated
Suspicious, vengeful or vindictive
Superb in temperament and emotionally loving
No trait of arrogance or selfish ambitions
Coexists with grace and returns hate with love
Friend and guide to everyone
Responds to the indwelling Spirit and
By the spiritual fruits serves mankind with nourishment for
Those who hunger and thirst for righteousness – for God
Impels the souls of men to believe by faith
To seek in the service of the kingdom of Heaven
The truth of the new gospel of the kingdom that:
Men and Women are the living spirit sons and daughters of the Eternal Father
Proclaimed that only by faith so can you be accepted entry
Into the new service of the Kingdom of Heaven
To partake for a life of loving service of your brothers and sisters in the flesh
If you: Extoll goodness, exalt beauty, preach devotion, teach reverence, and display loyalty
And, are you as wise as a serpent and as harmless as a dove?
Then you are indeed, Personality itself.

OF BEING

With a thankful gratitude
Not too clever nor cute
In your chosen stillness
Error is replaced by truth

Where harmony and ecstasy
Unclutters the mind
Within there is
Outside, no sign

In the unmistaken reality
As you listen and learn
Embodied in Spirit
Blessings, you earn

Manifest your field of consciousness
In happiness, remaining sane
In the existence of True reality
Where Divine truth rein

Through grace, beauty, love and joy
Life's meaning is worth seeing
Within your heart soul and mind
Is, the conscious experience
Of being.

www.ingramcontent.com/pod-product-compliance
Lightning Source LLC
LaVergne TN
LVHW061559070526
838199LV00077B/7107